The Next Voice You Hear

To Karen

and Shirley

and Chris

and Andy

and the folks at

Christ Presbyterian Church

in Terra Linda

The Next Voice You Hear

Sermons We Preach Together

David Steele

Geneva Press
Louisville, Kentucky

Book design by Sharon Adams
Cover design by Kevin Darst

First edition
Published by Geneva Press
Louisville, Kentucky

This book is printed on acid-free paper that meets the American National Standards Institute Z39.48 standard. ♾

PRINTED IN THE UNITED STATES OF AMERICA

Library of Congress Cataloging-in-Publication Data

99 00 01 02 03 04 05 06 07 08 — 10 9 8 7 6 5 4 3 2 1

Steele, David, 1931–
    The next voice you hear : sermons we preach together / David Steele. — 1st ed.
        p.   cm.
    ISBN 0-664-50040-4 (alk. paper)
    1. Presbyterian Church—Sermons   2. Sermons, American.
3. Choral recitations.   I. Title.
BX9178.S77N48   1999   99-11360
252'.051—dc21   CIP

CONTENTS

PREFACE

For eighteen years, I was parson of a community whose life together was defined and energized by weekly common worship. Whereas many churches grow by first making contact with people through support groups or study classes, Christ Presbyterian Church in Terra Linda, San Rafael, California, was the opposite. We discovered people first came to our church for worship and then joined a group or class.

We gathered weekly around a large communion table in a room with excellent acoustics for singing. We were blessed with top-notch musicians who not only provided rich vocal and instrumental music but operated out of the conviction that the congregation is the basic choir for Reformed worship. How the rafters rang with the mighty hymns of the church!

Guest preachers would often comment on something I discovered in my first few weeks with these folks. When a person stood up front, *you could sense the congregation rooting for you.* I called the phenomenon "positive vibes." A wonderful charismatic gentleman who was more conservative than I worshipped with us for several years because, as he put it, "The Spirit is present in this place!" His description is probably more accurate than mine.

Because worship was clearly a community event, it was natural for the sermon to move out beyond the pulpit. We began to experiment with ways preaching could be done with more than one voice. In the process, we found ourselves confronting God's Word in a different way. Instead of the somewhat didactic, professorial model where the robed figure up front tells us what a certain Bible passage means, we found ourselves as a congregation in the midst of the Word. We were entering into the Bible passage and discovering together how it touched our lives. Preaching became a community activity.

This book contains some of the sermons we preached together. They are arranged according to the movement of the church year. They are meant to be read out loud and thus are arranged on the paper in poetic form. With one or two rehearsals, lay folks can present these sermons very well.

The sermons were first preached by just plain folk. At Christ Church, I most often would sit up front on what we came to term the "liturgical stool," using a music stand for the script. The second voice would use the pulpit. We did not try to memorize.

Most of the sermons have been used in settings beyond Christ Church. The "Prodigal Son" and "Where Are the Other Nine?" have been presented in half a dozen worship services. The Communion drama "At the Table" appeared in a national magazine one Lent, and forty churches around the country wrote me to say they used it and found it very touching.

These experiences of the Word brought to me and the community of Christ Presbyterian Church in Terra Linda many moments of Amazing Grace. Grace can't be paid back; it must be passed on. And so we entrust them to you and your congregation.

Shalom,

David Steele

While the liturgical church year begins with Advent, every pastor knows the actual church year starts the Sunday after Labor Day. Vacations are over, school starts, and the congregation begins anew both program and mission. There are many tasks ahead. Who will help?

The following can be done with two readers up front and the other participants sitting in their regular seats (when their line comes, they stand and shout it out). The names and excuses in the text are those of real folks. A congregation may wish to revise their lines to fit the actual people speaking.

HERE I AM . . . SEND CLAUDE   5 min.

Exodus 3:1–12; 4:13

Reader 1   The thing about burning bushes is
            They get our attention!
            It's not that Yahweh God
            Loves showing off,
            Or anything like that.

Reader 2   "For my next trick, I present . . .
            A burning bush!"

Reader 1   Burning bushes come in many forms,
            In all sizes and shapes.
            We are going about our own business,
            Like Moses there at Horeb,
            And suddenly our attention is captured . . .

Reader 2   By the number of homeless ones in town,
            Or the treatment of the misfit at work,
            Or the weeds in the church garden,

Or the suffering of a good friend,
Or whatever . . .

Reader 1   We see a need.
By George, someone ought to do something!
Golly, someone has got to start caring!
We can stand it no longer;
The problem cannot be ignored.
It will not go away by itself.
Something must be done.

And lo and behold, we are there,
Standing at our burning bush.
God has captured our attention,
Pinpointed a particular need.
At work . . . in the neighborhood . . . at church . . .
In the family . . . in the world . . .
Someone has to start doing something!
That is clear at burning bushes.

But who is going to do it?
That is not so clear.
Who will tackle the job?
This is the part of the message
We have trouble understanding.
The need is clear,
But the name we keep hearing,
As we stand by that bush,
The name of the doer God has in mind,
Must be a mistake.
It is our own name.

Reader 2   Moses! Moses!

Reader 1   Here I am.

Reader 2   Moses, go down to Egypt Land;
            Tell old Pharaoh,
            To let my people go.

Reader 1   Right, Lord, something must be done in Egypt;
            Someone must help your people there.
            Thank goodness you see the need.
            It is about time you got around to acting.
            Congratulations, Lord. I'm all for the project.
            Here I am, Lord,
            But send Dottie.

Dottie   Here I am, Lord,
            But I am already serving on three important
                committees;
            Send Gladene.

Gladene   Here I am, Lord,
            But I have a house full of reweaving to finish;
            Send Carol.

Carol   Here I am, Lord,
            But working full time,
            And running a hotel for relatives,
            Is all I can do;
            Send Dave.

Dave   Here I am, Lord,

But I'm completely tied up in the World Wide Web;
Send Sue.

Sue   Here I am, Lord,
         But I've got to find a job;
         Send Bill.

Bill   Here I am, Lord,
         But it is not in my job description;
         Send Claude.

All   Who's Claude?

Reader 2 Here I am . . . Send Claude!
          It is natural, one supposes,
          To feel somewhat inadequate
          When confronting burning bushes.
          It is natural, one supposes,
          When we really have our attention
          Directed to a crucial need in human life,
          To feel our own resources
          Are not sufficient.

Reader 1 At burning bushes, we empathize with Moses,
          As he shouts out . . .

Reader 2 I am not religious enough for this job, Lord.
          I can't go to Egypt; I'm a wanted man there.
          I am not a public speaker.
          Here I am, but
          Dottie is friendlier;
          Send her.

Dottie   Gladene is more conscientious;
            Send her.

Gladene   Carol has been a member longer;
            Send her.

Carol   Dave is taller;
            Send him.

Dave   Sue has seminary training;
            Send her.

Sue   Bill has more experience;
            Send him.

Bill   Here I am, Lord;
            Send Claude.

All   Who's Claude?

Reader 1   The trouble with burning bushes is
            They don't go away.
            At burning bushes, we see a need.
            We hear our names being called.
            We may feel inadequate.
            We may be sure someone else could do it better.
            We may not want to be bothered.
            We wish the bush would go away,
            But burning bushes are very personal;
            That burning bush is for me.

Reader 2   Not Dottie,
            Not Gladene,
            Not Carol,
            Not Dave,
            Not Sue,
            Not Bill,
            Not Claude . . .

Reader 1   The burning bush I meet is my own.
            It is my name I hear called.
            There God calls me
            To meet the particular human need I see.
            No matter how I try to escape,
            The name that is called remains the same.

Reader 2   Moses! Moses!

Reader 1   It is my name.

Reader 2   Moses! Moses!

Reader 1   Here I am; send Dottie.

Dottie   Send Gladene.

Gladene   Send Carol.

Carol   Send Dave.

Dave   Send Sue.

Sue   Send Bill.

Bill   Send Claude.

All   Who's Claude?

Reader 1   But the burning bush is not for Claude;
             It is for me.
             Claude has his own bush.
             The bush I see,
             The need God puts before my eyes,
             In my mind,
             On my heart,
             Has my name written on it,
             And mine alone.

Reader 2   "And I heard the voice of the Lord saying,
             'Whom shall I send,
             and who will go for us?'
             Then I said, 'Here I am! Send me!'"

Postscript: The folks at Christ Church were captivated by Claude. Coffee-hour discussion led to an agreement that the reason things were not getting done around the church was that we were waiting for Claude to do them and that Claude was letting us down.

The following Sunday, a pair of overalls was hung in the narthex. The donor explained these were Claude's overalls. If we saw something that needed doing around the church—for example, cleaning dirty windows or messy bathrooms—we might write it down and put the note in Claude's overall pocket. Perhaps he would get around to doing it.

Others of us who felt we might have time to assist Claude might take a note from his pocket and do the job for him. Folks had fun with this for a while.

We eventually realized that we needed a more organized approach to assisting Claude with the work of the church. So, each September, we presented to members of the church a "Claude List,"—consisting of all the church jobs that needed doing. Folks indicated how much they planned to assist Claude in the coming year.

It worked!

Naaman the Syrian gives a contemporary twist to the biblical story. It easily becomes point 1 in a stewardship sermon. The choir makes a great chorus if they are willing and able. The chorus speaks in a rap beat. (Make up your own.) The last two lines of each chorus are read by a single voice.

NAAMAN THE SYRIAN

2 Kings 5:1–14

Chorus   I'm achin' to do something marvelous.
Lord, do you need a leader for an Exodus?
I'd like to get started on some great big thing
Like Mother Teresa or Martin Luther King.
I'll give my all without complaint,
To any task worthy of a saint.
Got a big job, Lord? I'm your nominee!
Here I am, Yahweh; please send me!

Voice 1   That's something big, Lord. Note: I'm not speakin'
'Bout teachin' Sunday school or serving as a deacon.

Reader   Naaman is pacing to and fro
In front of Elisha's bungalow.
Checking his watch, now fro, now to,
As "important" people tend to do
When life lets them know how a commoner feels.
(Generals aren't used to cooling their heels.)
Wouldn't a person like Naaman expect
A second-rate prophet to show more respect?
Naaman is mighty impatient, that's true.
Strange, this general has nothing better to do.

You see, he's a leper; and when his big "L"
Becomes public, that ends it. He bids fond farewell
To everything Naaman holds precious and dear.
His family, his comrades . . . his brilliant career.
Gone! He'll be banned to that dread quarantine
Reserved for the damned, the forever unclean.

To the prophet Elisha, this man of great wealth
Has come begging and pleading, praying for health.
It's his only hope and it's looking grim,
For the prophet is clearly ignoring him.
Then at last comes a servant bearing this word:
"Go wash in the Jordan. Your flesh will be cured."
"And?" queries Naaman. "And nothing. That's it!"
That does it for Naaman; he's ready to quit.

"I come seeking Elisha. I beg him to pray
For God's healing presence. I'm willing to pay!
And he won't even give me the time of day.
I ask for a prophet. I end up with *him*.
A lackey, who tells me to go take a swim.
We've great rivers in Syria, big, rushing ones, pal;
Beside them, your Jordan is just a canal.
For three weeks, I've followed the pilgrimage path,
For this! A servant suggests that I go take a bath!"

Chorus   I'm achin' to do something marvelous.
Lord, do you need a leader for an Exodus?
I'd like to get started on some great big thing,
Like Mother Teresa or Martin Luther King.
I'll give my all without complaint,

To any task worthy of a saint.
Got a big job, Lord? I'm your nominee!
Here I am, Yahweh. Please, send me!

Voice 2   I'll slay a dragon . . . eat raw liver!
But I won't go near that Jordan River.

Reader   Feeling the prophet's made light of his trust,
Naaman is ready to leave in disgust,
Till a servant says, "Father, O friend of the King,
If the prophet had asked you to do some great thing,
You would see it was done with nary a thought.
So . . . go wash in the Jordan? Tell me, why not?"
Why not indeed?
Great was his need.
And that dip in the Jordan, far from appealing,
Became the occasion for Naaman's healing.

Chorus   I'm achin' to do something marvelous.
Lord, do you need a leader for an Exodus?
I'd like to get started on some great big thing,
Like Mother Teresa or Martin Luther King,
I'll give my all without complaint,
To any task worthy of a saint.
Got a big job, Lord? I'm your nominee!
Here I am, Yahweh; please send me!

Voice 3   I get your point, Yahweh. I see when you call
I better be ready to do something small.

*The scripture is read by the reader. Since the two brothers
are male, a female reader adds voice contrast. The brothers
go after each other with vim and vigor. When the younger
brother sings "Amazing Grace," he does so with gusto.*

8 min. THE PRODIGAL SON

Luke 15:11—32 (RSV)

Reader   "Now, his elder son was in the field; and as he came
and drew near to the house, he heard music and
dancing. And he called one of the servants and
asked what this meant. And he said to him, 'Your
brother has come, and your father has killed the fatted calf, because he has received him safe and
sound.' But he was angry and refused to go in."

Junior   Dad says you aren't coming in.
Please . . . join us. Don't do this to him.

Senior   To him! Look what he's done to me!
You dishonor our family,
Waste your inheritance on whores,
And when you come sneaking home
The old man puts on a banquet.
The fatted calf no less.
I never got a dinner.
All these years and not so much as a goat.
It's disgusting!

Junior   Please . . . don't cut yourself off like this.
Dinner is just about ready.

Senior   We never talked!

Reader   "There was a man who had two sons; and the
           younger of them said to his father, 'Father, give me
           the share of property that falls to me.' And he di-
           vided his living between them."

Senior   That's the way it started; the whole thing made no
               sense.
Junior   He never did get what was going on—from the very
               start he . . .
           (*The brothers speak at the same time. They notice, and
           both stop; then the younger brother speaks.*)

Junior   Pardon me, brother.
           The firstborn always must have precedence.
           You were saying?

Senior   I can't understand why Dad did it.
           He and Mom have scrimped and saved to pay off the
               mortgage.
           The ranch is a good family business.
           Dad and I have worked our tails off here.
           That kid has never shown any interest.
           He doesn't know how to put in a day's work;
           Half the time, he's off carousing with his friends.
           We're carrying him.
           If you ask me, Dad ought to lay down the law,
           Get Junior to shape up . . . or else.
           But what does Father do?
           He borrows on the property
           To get the cash to give Junior his inheritance.
           And now his son is off to God-knows-where

With a big smile on his face
And lots of money in his jeans.
We are already short-handed;
What with me becoming more involved with the
    finances
And spending more time in the office.
Who's going to muck out the barn?
Who's going to fix the fences?

Junior   My brother obviously doesn't understand;
I doubt if he ever will.
He's top dog and will be till he dies.
Top dogs don't get how others feel.
That inheritance he talks about?
Do you know how that works?
As eldest, he inherits two-thirds.
That means he controls the ranch;
He's the head honcho
And will be till he dies.
What good is my third around here?
I'm going to work for him all my life.
That's what I told Dad.
Can you see how I feel, Father?
I'll always be second banana around here.
Put in my whole life,
And my obituary will read:
"He was so and so's brother."

I want to be my own man.
Can't you see that, Dad?
My own person . . . I can't do that around here.

Give me my inheritance.
Let me see what I can do on my own!

Reader   "So he divided his property between them."

Senior   Dad caved in.
           The act of a father turned wimp.

Junior   An act of respect for a son.

Senior   Oh?
           And what happened next?

Reader   "The younger son gathered all he had and took his
           journey into a far country, and there he squandered
           his property in loose living. And when he had spent
           everything, a great famine arose in that country, and
           he began to be in want. So he went and joined him-
           self to one of the citizens of that country, who sent
           him into his fields to feed swine. And he would
           gladly have fed on the pods that the swine ate; and
           no one gave him anything."

Junior   I'm sure you have some helpful commentary.

Senior   Yes, I do.
           That whole sorry mess was no surprise to me.
           All your life you have flitted around like a butterfly.
           You never learned how to work.
           You acted as though money grew on trees.
           Dad might have just as well set fire to that money,

And used the flames for barbecue,
As give it to you.
I knew you couldn't handle it.
He knew how irresponsible you were.
Why did he let you have that money?

Junior   Perhaps, so I could learn.
It was my inheritance, remember that.
I learned quite a bit.

Reader   "But when he came to himself he said, 'How many
of my father's hired servants have bread enough and
to spare, but I perish here with hunger! I will arise
and go to my father, and I will say to him, "Father, I
have sinned against heaven and before you; I am no
longer worthy to be called your son; treat me as one
of your hired servants." ' "

Senior   So that is the way you become your own man.
It certainly is impressive.
Your money is gone.
Do you take your licking like a man?
No way! You come running home whining.
With your tail between your legs.
Home to daddy . . .
And *that* is being responsible?

Junior   You have never really failed, have you?
You have no idea how that hurts,
To feel no damn good, day after day,
Week after week . . .

You have no idea how hard it is to admit it.
Then to say it aloud:
"I am not worthy!"
To realize that is the only thing
You can say about yourself:
"I am not worthy!"
When that happens,
If you have a home,
You head for it.

Reader   "Home is the place where, when you have to go
          there, they have to take you in. A place somehow
          you haven't to deserve!"

Junior   When you are not worthy,
          Home is your only hope.

Reader   "He arose and came to his father. But while he was yet
          at a distance, his father saw him and had compassion,
          and ran and embraced and kissed him. And the son
          said to him, 'Father, I have sinned against heaven and
          before you; I am no longer worthy to be called your
          son.' But the father said to his servants, 'Bring quickly
          the best robe, and put it on him; and put a ring on his
          hand and shoes on his feet; and bring the fatted calf
          and kill it, and let us eat and make merry; for this my
          son was dead, and is alive again; he was lost, and is
          found.' And they began to make merry."

Junior   (sings) Amazing Grace, how sweet the sound
          That saved a wretch like me.

I once was lost but now am found,
Was blind, but now I see.

| Senior | What have you done, Father?
Has this stopped being a moral universe?
Acts no longer have consequences?
Are we now to reward laziness,
Praise foolishness,
Encourage moral degradation,
Honor sin?
Your son has dishonored you,
Brought shame to our family,
Lost all your money.
Wallowed in immorality,
And this is cause for a party?
If he had committed murder,
I suppose, we'd be taking him to the circus? |

| Junior | (*sings*) Amazing Grace, how sweet the sound
That saved a wretch like me . . . |

| Senior | Listen to him, Father;
He's happy as a clam.
So he blew the money,
So he made fools of us all,
It doesn't matter.
Hey, he slinks home.
And, *voila*, the fatted calf!
He's sucked you into his irresponsibility, Dad.
You are codependent.
You've rescued him again, Father. |

Shielded him from consequences,
All in the name of love.
That is not love, Father;
Real love is tough.
It makes us face the music.
"Bring out the best robe!
Kill the fatted calf!"
That is not love, Father!
It is sentiment!
It is not what he deserves!

Junior   And he is right, of course,
It is not what I deserve.
Life does not always give us what we deserve.
The top dogs don't see that . . .
Or rather, don't want to see it.
When you are on top, and the system works for you,
Then you want to believe you deserve good fortune.
Top dogs are convinced their dedication,
Their hard work, their cleverness,
Their skill, their righteousness
Have earned them privilege, fame, or fortune!
But alas, arrives eventually the day
When ill fortune comes,
And we begin to understand
That tragedy oft comes to those who least
        deserve it.
And what can we say then?
Except, thank God,
The same is true of Grace.
Grace comes to us who don't deserve it.

Grace comes to us who least deserve it.
(*sings*)
I once was lost but now am found
Was blind and now I see.

Reader   "Now his elder son was in the field; and as he came
          and approached the house, he heard music and
          dancing . . . But he was angry and refused to go in.
          His father came out and entreated him . . ."

Senior   Lo, these many years I have served you, Father.
          I have never disobeyed your command.
          Yet, never . . . not once,
          Did you give me so much as a goat,
          So I could party with my friends.
          But now this son of yours returns,
          The one who has devoured your living with harlots,
          And you kill, *for him*, the fatted calf.
          I don't deserve this sort of treatment, Father.

Reader   And the father said to him, "Son, you are always
          with me, all that is mine is yours. It is fitting to make
          merry and be glad, for this your brother was dead
          and is alive. He was lost, and is found."

Senior   It's a disgrace!

Junior   No, it is Amazing Grace!

"Good King Asa" and "Baldy" highlight little-known biblical events. They may be more useful in education classes or church suppers than in morning worship—but an occasional snicker from the person in the pulpit is often appreciated. These could be illustrations in a sermon or perhaps used with children. While written for one voice, they can be read effectively with two.

GOOD KING ASA

I Kings 15:9–24

King Asa is scriptures' premier palindrome.
You'd think Bible students from Natchez to Nome
Would chortle with glee as they point out the stunt
How his name spells the same from the back or the front.
And some, of course, do, although more of them might;
For our knowledge of Asa is frightfully slight.
From the little we know, he gets bouquets and cheers
For his wise rule of Judah for forty-one years.

Asa mounted that throne in a gutsy way, brother.
He threw out the rascals, including his mother,
Who was not really worthy of Dowager Queen.
So he gave her the ax! (Guess you know what I mean.)
That Asa's some guy! So what happened next?
We're really not sure; there is too little text
Allotted to Asa. We simply are told
That his feet got diseased as King Asa grew old.

Did he come limping home every night as do we,
Moaning, "These dogs of mine are just killing me"?
Had he athlete's foot, an excess of starches

Causing bunions and corns? Was it fallen arches?
What caused good King Asa on that royal seat
To spend most of his time massaging his feet?
We know not. Our knowledge of Asa is slight.
Maybe he just wore his shoes "way too tight"!

Asa now may be serving a heavenly role
As the patron saint of Dr. Scholl.

BALDY

2 Kings 2:23–25

One supposes the teen Elisha bore a shaggy mane
   growing like well-fertilized sod;
But, alas, the mature prophet could but look in the
   mirror and wail, "I have thinned and fall short
   Of the glory of God!"

And as his hair grew thin,
So did his skin.

Thus, the "small boys" of whom the author of
   2 Kings 2:24 makes mention
Were ill advised to bring his scalp to the prophet's
   attention
By jeering, "Baldy, Baldy, Baldy!" How they teased!
To put it mildly, Elisha was far from pleased.
We read, "He cursed them in the name of the Lord"
   (as prophets will,
Though in this case, it sounds like overkill;
Especially when at that moment there was a growly
   noise).
"Then, two she-bears came out of the woods and mauled
   forty-two of the boys."
So reads Holy Writ.
That's it!

Forty-two boys! No less, no more?
Who kept score?
She-bears! Where were the He's?
At work? At ease?

So many questions . . . 'Tis a mystery, we fear,
Though one point is crystal clear;
Should you or I find our preacher's shiny dome amusing,
   we dare not snicker or share it.
Lest he fail to grin and bear it.

The parable of the vineyard uses a reader and chorus. The chorus sings its lines to the tune of the "Tallis Canon." The chorus sings lustily with great vigor. The choir might serve as the chorus. It would be appropriate on the fourth chorus to sing the words as a round to convey the feeling of the workers' contentment. It has been a satisfying day's work. A denarius represents top wages. What could be better?

THE VINEYARD LABORERS

Matthew 20:1–16

Reader   At 6:00 a.m., he came apace
To the daily labor hiring place.
"Care to work my field? I'll pay
A denarius at end of day."

Indeed they would! It had been ages
Since someone offered such fine wages.
They all were in that field ere long
Their voices raised in grateful song:

Chorus   (*sings to the tune "Tallis Canon"*)
'Tis joy to labor on this day,
To work for such outstanding pay.
The sun is warm, my muscles thrive.
It's such a treat to be alive!

Reader   At 9:00 a.m., at noon, and 3:00,
More folk beneath the labor tree
Were hired at the going rate.
They, too, agreed the pay was great.
They labored midst the vines ere long
Their voices raised in thankful song:

Chorus   (*sings*) 'Tis joy to labor on this day,
           To work for such outstanding pay.
           The sun is warm, my muscles thrive.
           It's such a treat to be alive!

Reader   But now the tale moves from sublime
           To ridiculous—near quitting time.
           For then, the owner, overjoyed,
           Finds other people unemployed.
           "Come, work my fields, and I will pay
           A full denarius today."
           And they joined in the work, ere long
           Their voices raised in cheerful song:

Chorus   (*sings*) 'Tis joy to labor on this day,
           To work for such outstanding pay.
           The sun is warm, my muscles thrive.
           It's such a treat to be alive!

Reader   All worked those vines with care, with love
           While giving thanks to God above
           For sending them this saint, this sage
           Who pays a decent living wage.
           They thanked their thoughtful boss for seeing
           Each worker as a human being.
           That night, each would stand tall on earth
           For they had earned what they were worth!
           Contentedly, at close of day
           They gathered to receive their pay.

Chorus   (*sings; may be sung as a round*)
            'Twas joy to labor on this day,
            To work for such outstanding pay.
            The sun is warm, my muscles thrive.
            It's such a treat to be alive!

Reader   And so according to his plan
            The owner paid to every man
            What each agreed was top-rate pay.
            A full denarius that day.
            And every person was content
            Until they saw this pay scale meant
            The workers who the owner met
            So late they barely raised a sweat
            Were paid the same as those who'd born
            The vineyard work since early morn.
            The early workers gathered there
            Were angry, for it seemed unfair.

Chorus   (*sings angrily*) We broke our backs; we slaved today.
            And all for this! Such stingy pay.
            You paid the ones who came at four
            The same as us—we should get more!

Reader   Aghast at how their joy had fled,
            The owner turned to them and said,
            "We both agreed, at break of day,
            A denarius is princely pay.
            All day you were a happy crew.
            Till all were paid the same as you.
            And now you sigh. You moan and groan.

Does your friends' good fortune diminish your
   own?"

So it appears,
One fears.
A denarius for me will do,
Till I perceive you have one too.

This simple musical is effective at Thanksgiving worship. It is appropriate for a stewardship dinner. The Rev. Karen Stokes wrote the lyrics and I the narration. The tunes are familiar. You will note the Samaritan here is a woman. We felt this added to the drama. This sermon requires a reader and chorus. The chorus includes all the speakers and singers. The musical needs to be well rehearsed, but when the congregation joins the cast at the end, the result is very moving and well worth the effort.

WHERE ARE THE OTHER NINE?

by Karen Stokes and David Steele

Reader	(*Opens the pulpit Bible and reads Luke 17:11—17*) (*substitute* she *for* he *in v. 15–16*)
Chorus	(*The overture*) (*Tune: Theme from "Gilligan's Island"*)
All	(*Sing*) Now sit right back, and you'll hear a tale A tale of a dread disease That turns all kinds of normal folks Into refugees. It doesn't matter who they were Before the sickness came; Once you're a leper, you'll never lead A normal life again.
Solo 1	(*sings*) One day, in a village near Galilee, On a hot and dusty street, Ten lepers cried to passersby For a crust of bread to eat.

Solo 2　　(*sings*) They saw a man coming up the road
　　　　　　With a ragged, dusty band;
　　　　　　The rumors said he could raise the dead
　　　　　　With a wave of his hand!

All　　　　(*sing*) With a wave of his hand!
　　　　　　They didn't dare get close to him,
　　　　　　For that was not allowed . . .

Solo 3　　(*sings*) "Have mercy on us, please, my Lord,"
　　　　　　They cried above the crowd.

Solo 2　　(*sings*) "Go show yourself to the priests," he said,
　　　　　　And then he moved along.

All　　　　(*sing*) "Well, what the heck?"
　　　　　　They shrugged and said,
　　　　　　"There's nothing left to go wrong."
　　　　　　They headed down the road, and saw
　　　　　　Their leprosy was gone!

Reader　　(*speaks*) They stand there, dumbfounded,
　　　　　　Those chosen ten.
　　　　　　Bewildered, elated,
　　　　　　The women, the men,
　　　　　　Near the Office of Health
　　　　　　(The Jerusalem branch),
　　　　　　For they have been handed
　　　　　　A second chance
　　　　　　To live, to love,
　　　　　　To make their mark,

Here in the sunshine,
Called out of the dark,
Gone their disease!
Now normal, and clean,
'Tis the grandest day
They have known or seen,
Fresh, brand-new,
Like the morn of creation.
Their hearts overflow
With exhilaration!
Now one steps forward,
Stands strong and tall.
Listen . . . She surely
Must speak for them all.

Samaritan (*sings to the tune "Unforgettable"*)
Unacceptable
In every way.
"Unacceptable!"
That's what they'd say.

I could hardly even bear it then,
Both a leper and Samaritan!
You came along,
Said they had it wrong!

Unacceptable?
That's not the case,
When you offer me
Amazing Grace!
I guess I'll just have to dare it then.

Still a woman, still Samaritan,
You say I can be acceptable, too!

(*Schmaltzy piano break*)

Thank you, Jesus! It's incredible
That someone so unforgettable
Thinks that I can be acceptable, too!

Samaritan (*speaks*) Friends,
We have shared with each other
The pain of disaster.
Let us travel, as one,
To bring thanks to the Master.

Reader   (*speaks*) But, even as she speaks,
Saul is bustling, nonstop,
To the street where he owns
A small furniture shop.
Convinced that his partner,
By some sort of slick
Double-entry, has robbed him,
When Saul was so sick.
He'll soon catch that skunk
Who has stolen him blind.
Revenge is the one thing
Saul has on his mind.
His partner may soon leave
The land of the living.
Saul has no interest
At all in thanksgiving.

(*Gong sounds*)

All   (*shout*) One!

Reader   (*speaks*) Oh . . . Oh!
          It appears Bartimaeus
          May not make that trip.
          He's under the date palm
          There, taking a nip.

Bartimaeus (*sings, to the tune "Roll Out the Barrel"*)
          Haul out the wineskins,
          We'll have a barrel of fun.
          I'm celebrating
          Something that someone has done.
          Some good thing happened,
          Something has me all a-buzz . . .
          Now, if I could just remember
          What that something was!

          Open the wineskin . . .
          That's what I always have done
          When I was lonely,
          And living wasn't much fun.
          Now someone healed me,
          Now I am happy, I think.
          I should prob'ly go and thank him,
          But I'd rather drink!

          (*Gong sounds*)

All   (*shout*) Two!

Reader   (*speaks*) Enter Mark's wife.
              She has heard the Good News.
              She comes with an offer
              Too good to refuse.
              The neighbors will care for the kids
              Till next noon,
              So they can take off
              On a brief honeymoon.
              Mark's grateful, of course,
              But the Master can wait.
              'Cause he and his honey
              Have got a big date.

              (*Gong sounds*)

All   (*shout*) Three!

Reader   (*speaks*) Now David speaks.

David   (*speaks*) I'd like to thank Jesus
              But you know, I
              Dare not go with you,
              I'm just too shy . . .
              And afraid to try.

              (*Gong sounds*)

All   (*shout*) Four!

Reader   (*speaks*) And Judah?
            No place for him
            Within the ranks
            Of any pilgrimage of thanks.

Judah   (*sings to the tune "Come, Ye Thankful People, Come"*)
            Why be thankful people, why?
            Just because we did not die?
            I got just what I deserve!
            Doesn't Jesus have some nerve?
            Don't you think he should explain
            Why I went through so much pain?
            I should bless the Lord today?
            That's easy for you to say!

            If the truth can now be said,
            I should *curse* the Lord instead.
            I have wasted half my life . . .
            Lost my children, lost my wife.
            That is *not* Amazing Grace!
            How would you feel in my place?
            So, you will excuse me, please,
            If I *don't* fall on my knees!

            (*Gong sounds*)

All   (*shout*) Five!

Reader   (*speaks*) Since Jonah looks healthy,
            Is feeling great, too,

He'd like to enroll
At Jerusalem U.
And today just happens
To be the last date
When all the new students
Must matriculate.
He'd like to see Jesus,
Maybe next year;
But, today, he begins
To pursue his career.

(*Gong sounds*)

All   (*shout*) Six!

Samaritan (*speaks*) Friends,
We have shared with each other
The pain of disaster.
Let us journey, as one,
To bring thanks to our Master.

Duet   (*Tune:* "*You've Got To Be Taught*")

Ruth   (*sings*) We ought to go back,
Along with her,
Give thanks for the things
That did occur;
For we are no longer
The scum that we were.
We ought to go back and say, "Thanks!"

Peter   (*sings*) You're probably right,
But think it through.

It could be a foolish
Thing to do.
What will people think,
If they see *her* with you,
If you should go back to say "Thanks!"

Ruth   (*sings*) When we were unclean,
She did help a lot.

Peter   (*sings*) She always would share
The food that she got.

Ruth   (*sings*) And all of the streetwise
Things that she taught.

Both   (*sing*) But now *we* are clean, and she's *not* . . .
(*spoken*) Samaritan people are *not*.

Ruth   (*sings*) It makes me feel bad
To think this way:
But I must agree
With what you say.
Perhaps it will all
Be better some day.
And then we'll go back and say, "Thanks!"

Both   (*sing*) Yes, then we'll go back and say, "Thanks!"

(*Gong sounds*)

All   (*shout*) Seven!

(*Gong sounds*)

All   (*shout*) Eight!

Reader   (*speaks*) Eight can't give thanks,
For one reason or other.
But Benjamin's left.
Look, here comes his mother.
She's wearing the latest
In fashion and dress,
And is surrounded by media types
From the press.

Mom   (*speaks*) We understand Benjamin . . .

Reader   (*speaks*) . . . *points to the boy* . . .

Mom   (*speaks*) . . . has been healed by some Jesus!
O, 'tis such a joy!
His father and I
Plan to do something pleasant
To show our gratitude
To that marvelous peasant.
Please tell this . . . *Jesus* . . .
We want him to know,
We'll discuss it this week
At our seaside chateau.
'Twill please that poor preacher,
Yes, give him a lift,
To hear he'll receive
A quite generous gift.

We're happy to do this,
We have no regret.
Our family proudly
Pays off every debt.
My husband is waiting,
We must hurry on.
Come along, Junior!

Reader   (*speaks*) He shrugs, and they're gone!

(*Gong sounds*)

All   (*shout*) Nine!

Reader   (*speaks*) Ten lepers healed,
            Yet, only one
            Returns, with thanks—
            The Samaritan!

Samaritan   (*sings to the tune of* "*Unforgettable*")
            Unacceptable,
            In every way.
            "Unacceptable!"
            That's what they'd say.
            I could hardly bear it then,
            Both a leper and Samaritan.
            You came along,
            Said they had it wrong!

All   (*sing*) Unacceptable?
            That's not the case

When you offer me
Amazing Grace!

Samaritan (*sings*) I guess I'll just have to dare it then.
Still a woman, still Samaritan.
You say I can be acceptable, too!

(*Instrumental bridge*)

All (*sing*) Thank you, Jesus! It's incredible
That someone so unforgettable
Thinks that I can be acceptable, too!

Reader (*speaks*) Then said Jesus:
"Were not ten cleansed?
Where are the other nine?"

Chorus (*sing*) Thank you, Jesus! It's incredible
and That someone so unforgettable
Congregation Thinks that I can be acceptable, too!

AN ADVENT POTPOURRI

*Most churches have special music during advent worship.
The twenty-minute sermon may not be the most effective
way of speaking the Word. Here is a collection of short
pieces that may be used during advent worship or dinners
or parties or whatever. They may be read separately or
combined to form a larger whole. Each packs a punch.*

The Vice-President
of Authentic Créches Speaks

The board turned down
My proposal to expand our top-of-the-line model
   (#G-41)
To include the events outlined in Matthew 2:16—18.

They agreed the addition of a soldier or two,
And a few bloody babies,
Would make #G-41 more authentic.
But it would spoil Christmas
And perhaps warp the psyches of our children,
To have an awful reminder of Herod's horror
There on the mantel next to the Baby Jesus.
The market probe provided the data:
Such a créche would never sell.

So, if my family, and yours
Wants to include the Slaughter of the Innocents
In our advent meditations,
We'll have to watch the evening news together.

I said to my pastor,
"It's still a good idea!

If we learned while very young
How to put the Savior and the slaughters together
There on the mantel . . .
Wouldn't we have a better chance
Of seeing how the Savior could touch
Our evening-news-world?
Trouble is,
The innocents are still out there being slaughtered,
While we keep the Savior safe on the mantel."

"That's an Easter issue," she said.

"Well, let's carve Easter créches!"

The Chair of the Bethlehem Chamber of Commerce Building Committee Speaks

We are excited
About the architect's preliminary plans for our civic
    memorial
Honoring the incarnation.
We could see at a glance,
How wise he has been
To suggest a hillside site, overlooking the city.
The vistas from *Meditation Portico*.
The olive groves, the grazing sheep, the little town
    below
Will be much more conducive to deep musings
On the mystery of the birth of the Child of God
Than any site we might try to pretty up
Around the stable in that rather seedy part of town.

Our board loves the overall concept.
The marble courtyard sets off the chapel well.
The space within is large enough to evoke
A sense of the majesty of God
    (and to accommodate several tour groups)
Without being dominating or oppressive.
Here is a sense of understated elegance
So appropriate for remembering the Holy Birth.
The snack bar and gift shop are readily accessible,
But do not intrude on the overall reverent ambiance.

But we do take issue on one point,
(And here we are agreed):
The focal center of the memorial,
There under the dome,
Cannot be, as the architect suggests,
Simply cannot be,
That ugly, rickety old animal-feeding trough!

We find that quite unacceptable.
It does not fit in.
Our committee prefers . . . a bronze cradle.

The Wisemen Speak

We love Matthew's Christmas story
And appreciate being included,
But as is so often true,
The reporter doesn't get the story quite right.

He senses our love of metaphor,
Hence our symbolic gifts: gold, frankincense, myrrh.

We bore regal gifts,
And presented them majestically
Matthew captures that moment well.

It is the high point of the pageant,
And makes a marvelous Christmas card.
We knew what we were doing.

Gifts fit for a king, to be sure,
But not for a baby
Or for his parents,
Alone, in great danger,
In a strange town . . . among strangers.

We knew they needed help.
We warned them about Herod.
Left Joseph a map, camels, a filled purse,
And a letter of introduction to the Magi community
     in Egypt.
Matthew missed that part.

So the way his story comes out,
We present the Baby those outlandish gifts
(About as practical as the Nieman Marcus
     catalog),
Then ride off into the sunset
And leave those kids to their own devices.

Give us a break.
We are intellectuals, true,
But we're not stupid!

A Grandparent Asks

Dr. Luke,
What about the others?
Participants in the nativity,
Ignored by you and your friends?

What of the parents?
Mary's . . . Joseph's . . .
Home in Nazareth,
While those kids take off for Bethlehem,
Sans reservations or credit cards.

Those pre-Ma Bell parents,
Worried . . . wondering . . .
On pins and needles.
What of them?

Did they get a star?
Or a company of angels singing:
"Unto us a child is born?
Unto us a grandson is given!"

They'd not need much.
A simple
"Mother, dad, and babe are doing fine!"
We grandfolks know
Our offspring's offspring surely is divine!

Matthew 2.2

The great thing about following stars
        is
It gets us out of the house.

Christmas Pageant

The cute little angel
Scrooched her brow
And tilted her head
As she proclaimed,
"Behold, I bring you good news of great joy!"
She looked angelic
But far from joyful.

It was her dang coat-hanger-halo,
Too tight, off center.

We caught the moral:
Halos are a headache!

Simeon

This preacher
Claimed scholarly research had documented
That Simeon,
Of Simeon and Anna,
Had pronounced the very same blessing
(The one in Luke 2:27–35)
Over all the babies presented to him in the Temple
Those final years of his life
(Around 5 B.C.)

He was pulling my leg, of course.

But, when I read the blessing
And thought about it,

I began to wish he was right,
About Simeon . . . and those babies.
And I began thinking about our babies.

And I wished someone,
Some Simeon,
Might hold my grandbabies high . . . and yours . . .
The born ones and the not yet . . .
Proclaiming to them with great conviction,
"You are the saviors of the world!"
Meaning it so absolutely
Those young'uns would live it,
And love it,
And make it happen!

Lent: These three "Were You There?" pieces may be used as a series or by themselves. Each looks at a participant in Jesus passion through contemporary eyes. The spiritual is a natural for just before or after the message.

WERE YOU THERE?

Caiaphas Speaks

Reader 1   As a religious, one does not seek authority.
But when one is called,
When hands are laid upon the head,
When matters of the purity of faith
Are placed within one's care . . .
That is a high and holy responsibility.
One dare not take it lightly.

It becomes necessary then,
To cut out and remove infection,
As one removes decay in an apple,
Or as a surgeon amputates the gangrenous limb
To save the patient's life.
The process may be bloody.
Surgery is not for the squeamish.
But when the health of the body of faith is at stake,
One must act! Quickly! Decisively!

Reader 2   It is sometimes pointed out
That the Galilean was a good man.
Upright, gentle . . . even, they say, loving.
That was never at issue.
He may have been kind to animals,
Never neglected to send a card on Mother's Day,

A good friend and neighbor.
He may have been very likable;
Heretics often are.
But one cannot permit charismatic teachers
To spread false doctrine,
Poisoning the minds and hearts of the faithful.
For the good of the faith,
And the sake of the faithful,
Such people, no matter how nice they are,
Must be silenced.
One cannot brood over moral character.

Reader 1   God knows, Jesus was warned.
From those early days,
When he first attracted attention,
He was under careful surveillance.
To be sure, it was difficult, at first,
To pinpoint his lack of orthodoxy.
So much of his teaching seemed based on the faith.
He often quoted the law and prophets,
Spoke of his love for Yahweh,
His respect for the covenant,
The glory of our chosen-ness.
He indicated a concern for fulfilling the law.
But then one noticed
How he dared place his personal opinion
Above our honored tradition.
"You have heard it said . . .
But I say unto you . . ."
He implied he spoke for Yahweh!
Such presumption cannot be tolerated.

Reader 2   One cannot permit the faithful
            To be exposed to the ideas
            Of every Tom, Dick, and Sarah.
            Those of us commissioned to protect the truth
            Must not allow error any rights.
            The minds and hearts of the faithful
            Must be sealed off . . . protected,
            Lest they be misled
            And wander down primrose paths to perdition.
            One must not allow God's revealed truth
            To be watered down with personal hunches.
            Jesus was warned.
            He was ordered time and time again
            To cease and desist his blasphemous teaching.
            He chose to ignore our counsel.
            The end was inevitable.

Reader 1   To be sure, we were mistaken
            In thinking a morals charge was in order.
            For a time it seemed likely
            He could be successfully eliminated as a moral
                deviate.
            His companions were surely sordid—
            Women with shady reputations,
            Publicans, public sinners . . .
            He had a penchant for riffraff.
            It was indeed disappointing
            When our investigators reported
            They could find not the slightest hint of moral
                indiscretion.
            Both he and the community about him

Proved cleaner than a hound's tooth.
The moral character of their life together
Was, in fact, exemplary.

Reader 2   Puzzling! In light
Of his clear encouragement of immorality.
His community routinely violated
The sacred laws of Sabbath.
He welcomed to his bosom
Collectors of the hated Roman tax,
Men who had for years feathered their own nest
At the expense of our own suffering people.
There was the case of the adulteress,
Clearly guilty of violating
The divinely appointed marriage covenant,
Tried, convicted publicly and openly,
And this Nazarene had the audacity
To intervene and subvert her just stoning.
"Let him who is without sin cast the first stone."
One cannot allow such sentimentality
To undermine Divine Justice.

Reader 1   Sentiment is not appropriate
When moral standards are at stake.
Surround that woman with all the sentiment
        you wish.
Imagine her husband a sadistic brute,
Stumbling home drunkenly night after night,
To batter his wife into semiconsciousness.
Suppose she at last finds a friend,
A man who feels for her, with her.

She turns to him for comfort,
Knows in his arms,
For the first time in her life,
Something of what the word *love* must mean . . .
Paint this woman with all the sentiment you
    choose
That does not alter the basic question:
Can society allow her adultery to go unpunished?
Indeed not . . . not if one hallows moral standards.

Reader 2   When one is entrusted by God and the community
To uphold covenant standards of morality,
One dares not allow sentiment to fog the issue.
Allow this woman to get off scot-free,
And others will claim they too
Can willfully violate the marriage bed.
The courts will be filled with women begging for
    mercy,
Trotting out the flimsiest of excuses,
Insisting they are entitled to an exception from
    the law.
Moral vision becomes cloudy, foggy;
No longer are folk able to discern clearly what is
    right
And what is wrong.
Moral life become chaotic . . . Anarchy reigns!
People end up doing what *feels* good,
What they *think* is right.
The commandments of Almighty God
Become a list of ten suggestions.
This cannot be permitted.

Reader 1   One wonders if the man was very bright.
             Some of the finest minds among us
             Oft tried in friendly debate,
             To help him understand the crucial role law plays
             In creating moral order, maintaining moral
                 standards.
             He responded with words about love.
             He had the gall to claim
             Our beloved commandments might be replaced
             By simply loving God with all one's heart
             And loving the neighbor as oneself.
             Talk about fuzzy thinking!
             Can you imagine junking our clear moral code
             And placing ourselves at the mercy
             Of what any Tom, Dick, or Jesus imagines to
                 be love?
             Love is too fuzzy, too slippery, too subjective.
             One cannot run a life or a society on love.
             That man had to go.

Reader 2   One trusts this puts to rest those nasty rumors
             That our condemnation of the false Messiah
             Was, at its core, a reaction to financial pressure.
             To be sure, we all were hard-pressed
             After his wild temple foray—
             Shouting, flailing his arms like a madman,
             Releasing expensive doves,
             Driving to the four winds precious cattle, lambs . . .
             Overturning money tables.
             Two days before Passover,
             And the man makes a shamble of Temple business,

On one of the biggest Temple days of the entire
    year!
No question many prominent people were upset.
Yes, we heard from them.
Yes, some threats about cutting pledges were made.
Yes, we were concerned about the financial
    implications
Of further Temple interruptions.
Perhaps this pressure did push us
To a more speedy trial and execution than was at
    first anticipated.
But the man was a goner . . .
Long before his Temple hi-jinks.

Reader 1   It is, after all, a heavy responsibility
            To serve on the Sanhedrin as temple trustees.
            The Galilean may praise the penny
            Placed in the offering box by a widow on welfare,
            But we cannot afford such luxuries.
            Running a temple requires substantial funding.
            One does not anger the geese that lay the golden
                eggs—
            Unless one is insane.

Reader 2   Nor will one take heed of that empty prattle:
            "Do you think institutions are more important than
                people?"
            Land sakes, the Temple is for and about people.
            Here we are dedicated to the Lord;
            Here we come for marriage;
            Here we come in times of joy, times of despair.

The Temple offers comfort and solace.
Here we find support, forgiveness, hope.
Every day God's needy ones gather outside the
    walls,
Waiting for the Temple gates to open.
Are we to tell them,
"Sorry, folks, the Temple will be open but three days
    a week
Until the Nazareth preacher ceases to annoy our
    hefty givers?"
No . . . that Galilean was a threat.
There was disease in the body of faith,
We excised it cleanly, quickly.
It was our responsibility
So to do.

Reader 1   One hoped, of course, this Galilean
              Might have recognized his error, owned up to
                  his crimes,
              As did, it is reported,
              One of the thieves who shared his hill that
                  Golgatha afternoon.
              One hoped for some sign of repentance.
              It was not forthcoming.
              One prays for the state of his immortal soul.

Reader 2   It is reported that during the ordeal of his dying
              He spoke as one close to Yahweh God,
              As a child moving through agony
              Toward a reunion with a parent.
              One wished for more . . .

One hoped he might see in that pain, his folly . . .
Cry aloud: "Father, forgive *me*."

Reader 1   Instead, he called out pathetically,
"Father, forgive *them*;
They know not what they do!"
Strange, misguided man . . .
We knew full well what we were doing.
We would do the same tomorrow.
When one is called,
When hands are laid upon the head,
When matters of the purity of faith
Are placed within one's care.
What else is one to do?

Pilate (A Colleague's Counsel)

Reader 1   My dear Pontius,
I was frankly overwhelmed by your letter.
Your openness and honesty are touching.
Indeed, I felt honored,
And more than a trifle humbled,
By the trust you have placed in me.
Yes, I had heard,
Mainly through the grapevine,
Rumors of your last few years—
Tales of your compulsive cleanliness,
Your tendency to withdraw from family and friends.
I am glad you understand my hope
That we two can get back in touch,
As the sincere wish of a friend

Rather than the curiosity of a nosy old man.
Your retirement is more troubled than you deserve.
Lord knows, we gave our best to the Emperor.
We are entitled to a time of ease in our senior years,
Surrounded by children and grandchildren.
A time of comfort, contentment, fulfillment,
I pray that for you.

Reader 2   You always were a brooder!
It is obvious that Galilean's fate
Has been running 'round and 'round in your mind,
Tossing and turning in your soul.
Remember how I used to say to you
When we were just schoolboys,
"Pontius," I'd say, "Pontius,
Stop chasing your tail and get back to living."
I say it to you once more
With a voice now cracking and tremulous,
But no less sincere.
"Pontius, you must stop chasing your tail."

Reader 1   At the time, none of us second-guessed you.
Oh, you may have received a slap on the wrist
From some second-rate clerk at headquarters,
But none of your colleagues was critical.
All of us with field command
Know how inane those stylus pushers can be.
It is one thing to write the directives:
"Provincial governors will not allow themselves
To be drawn into local political squabbles!"
It is quite another matter

When the fanatics are banging on your door
And the mobs fill the streets.
Believe me, friend, all of us in the provinces
Understood the pressures you faced.
You had our enthusiastic support.

Reader 2   You simply had rotten luck.
Jerusalem at Passover is a tinder box.
Always has been, always will be.
Those peasants from the country
Milling around their beloved Temple
Are tailor-made for manipulation by demagogues.
You were wise to be alarmed,
And concerned lest this incident
Erupt into violence and chaos.
We governors are paid to see
Business continues as usual,
And the camel trains run on time.
Your speedy action nipped the chaos in the bud,
Before it could spread into riot or revolution.
We in similar situations applauded your decisive
    action
And thanked whatever gods there be
The incident occurred on your watch
And not our own.

Reader 1   I admit I chuckled a bit at your predicament.
How many times did I warn you at the academy
That you might well balance your nightlife
With quite a bit more library time
If you hoped for a proper posting at graduation?

A more distinguished academic record
Might have spared you from an assignment among
    the Jews.
We did take some delight at your appointment.
It appeared to us you were paying for all those
    midnight hours
You spent in school among the ladies of the
    evening.
Not that we felt we could do better in Judea, or
    Galilee.
Those folk with their fanatical allegiance to
    their God
Are practically ungovernable.
Few of us could have done as well as you.

Reader 2   In retrospect, of course, it is natural
To wonder what might have happened
Had you played your cards differently.
Twenty/twenty hindsight is no great
    accomplishment.
If you had known this Jesus matter
Was more than just a typical struggle for power
Among rival Jewish sects,
You might have been more clever
In handling the Man and His disciples.
But how could you have known
He was not just another Jewish charismatic teacher?
Those fellows are a dime a dozen.
They blaze suddenly into popularity like a meteor,
And as quickly fizzle out . . . forgotten . . . of no
    consequence.

None of us had an inkling this Jesus might be
    different.
Yet he has proven to be.

Reader 1   The faith this Jesus inspires
             Has grown swiftly far beyond the bounds of Judaism.
             One find gatherings of these *Christians*
             In most of our larger cities,
             As well as scatterings among the country folk.
             The appeal of the Jesus faith does not appear to be
                 limited
             To a particular race, a social group, a cultural
                 tradition.
             These Christians are accomplishing
             What we in the Empire have yearned for but have
                 never quite achieved:
             A true unity of diverse peoples.
             One wonders if their leader
             Could have been co-opted by the state
             Rather than martyred.

Reader 2   It appears these *Christians* are not hostile
                 to government per se.
             Their most prominent leader, Saul of Tarsus,
             Speaks proudly of his Roman citizenship.
             He supports the civil order
             As being ordained by God,
             And urges his colleagues to be good citizens.
             Jesus himself is said to have urged his disciples,
             "To give Caesar what is Caesar's
             And God what is God's."

One wonders if this young faith
Could have been wooed more successfully by Rome,
And drawn into the service of the Empire.

Reader 1   Religion can provide a powerful bulwark for the state.
            When service to God and service to country are
                united,
            Powerful forces are unleashed on behalf of the state.
            The soldier who believes he fights for God
            Is worth a dozen mercenaries.
            The proper mix of God and country
            Creates loyal, devoted citizens.
            In retrospect, it now appears
            We badly underestimated Jesus and his followers.
            If only today we could harness their energy and
                devotion.

Reader 2   One wonders if it might have been to our advantage
            Had you played your cards differently in this Jesus
                matter.
            It is, of course, a judgment call.
            It depends, I suppose, on the sort of God
            This Christian God turns out to be.
            Our Roman gods have been quite malleable,
            Amenable to state control and manipulation.
            They have been easily co-opted into our state
                religions.
            But of course, our Roman gods have no power.
            By reducing our deities to state functionaries,
            We have rendered them impotent.
            Our faith no longer has much punch.

Reader 1   On the other hand, the Jewish God,
             Yahweh, I believe they call Him (or is it Her?),
             That Jewish God stands above and beyond
             Any and all human authority.
             We have tried every way we can imagine
             To get control of that God and its followers without
                 success.
             Yahweh God will not be controlled
             Yahweh God's effect on believers is so powerful,
             They cannot be effectively controlled either.
             Try as we might, we have not succeeded
             Lo these many years.

Reader 2   It appears we are confronted with Hobson's choice:
             "If a god is easy to control, the faith has no power;
             If a faith has power, its God cannot be controlled."
             Which God did you face at that trial?
             Was the God of Jesus
             More like Yahweh, or Jupiter?
             If only you had known then.
             Do you know now?

Reader 1   You must stop blaming yourself for what is done.
             The way out of your depression is the way through,
             And that means you must own up to the hand
                 washing.
             I must confess, when I first heard about it,
             I felt you were waffling.
             As we understood the story,
             You were convinced Jesus was a victim of trumped-
                 up charges.

You found him innocent of any capital crime.
As judge you were honor-bound to release him.
Yet you feared mob action, civil disorder,
Should you set the man free.
You had two choices:
As judge, set the innocent man free,
Or as governor, order the execution of him as a
    threat to public safety.
Either action may be defended and respected.

Reader 2   But when you took the bowl
And claimed to wash your hands of the decision,
Well, Pilate, that was a dodge of the first order.
The decision was yours to make.
You made it.
Own that decision; face up to it; claim it as your
    own.
This wimpy hand washing with the claim
That you did not make the decision . . .
"They did," you are reported to have said.
My friend, *not* to decide is to decide.
You cannot blame your life on some nebulous "they."
You rendered that verdict.
Say it to yourself, to another person, out loud:
"I did it. I ordered Jesus' execution!"
Only when you own this act
Will you find strength to move beyond it.

Reader 1   I am almost tempted to quote to you
Some of the teachings of the man you martyred that
    Passover morn.

He spoke of a God who loves, forgives, sets people
    free.
I find myself strangely attracted to him and his ideas
As I reflect upon my life in retirement.
It would be presumptuous of me
To thrust his words upon you.
But I commend them to you.
There are scrolls now in circulation
Which contain the story of Jesus and his ministry.
You may find their reading a source of inspiration
    and new life.
It is ironic, to be sure,
But I believe it may be true:
The man you sentenced to death
May, at last, become the source of your salvation.

Judas, the Betrayer

Preacher   "Then, one of the twelve,
            Who was called Judas Iscariot,
            Went to the chief priests and said,
            'What will you give me,
            If I deliver Jesus to you?'
            And they paid him thirty pieces of silver.
            And from that moment he sought an opportunity to
            betray Him."

            An awful story . . .
            A sorry specimen of humanity!

Advocate   Or a misunderstood, maligned one!

Preacher Judas? But the record is clear, consistent . . .
          He was the betrayer,
          The treasurer of the disciples,
          Whose greed led him to that unholy bargain.
          "For thirty pieces of silver
          I will betray my Master with a kiss."
          It's all here in Matthew, Mark . . . in Luke and John.
          There is no question of the record.

Advocate Unless one asks, who compiled this sorry record?
          Where did it come from?
          From persons who were bewildered, distraught,
              hurt.
          People in shock over the tragic events of Holy
              Week.
          Disciples grasping for some simple answer.
          "Why did one of us turn him in?
          Why? Why? Why?
          We trusted Judas; He trusted Judas.
          He was a hard worker . . . kept scrupulous
              accounting of our funds.
          That must be it!
          He knew money; he loved money,
          And he saw a way to quick cash.
          So he betrayed our Lord for filthy lucre!"

          That's your record.

Preacher It is. And . . .

Advocate It's too simple. Too cut and dried.
          That's not the way people act.

That's not the way history happens.
We have a record compiled by people grasping at
    straws.

Preacher   Perhaps . . .
But why your concern?
Who are you?

Advocate   An advocate . . . *amicus curiae*,
Concerned, lest judgments made under stress
Blacken the name, the memory,
Of one whom Jesus honored with the title
    disciple!

Preacher   Why now? Why here?
Our theme is not about Judas.
It is, "Were you there?"
The theme is about us.
Were we . . . are we . . . there at the cross?

Advocate   Precisely why I am here as Judas's advocate.
Make him a straw man,
As the evangelists have done,
And he is easy to dismiss as one inherently evil;
A miser motivated by malignant greed.
We'll not give a second thought to such a cardboard
    villain.
We would never put on his sandals,
Nor will he wear our Nikes.

Preacher   But, the record is clear . . .

Advocate It's far from convincing.
Take the money—thirty pieces of silver.
It is just not enough.
That's the price of a slave in the Old Testament,
Barely, twenty dollars.

Preacher There's disagreement on that point, you know.
Some scholars claim it was much more.
The wages for 120 days of manual labor, they say.
It all depends into what sort of coin
Those thirty pieces of silver were made.

Advocate That's still not enough to matter.
Look, this man knew money.
If greed is his motive,
Embezzlement is a much wiser and safer path.
He could palm double that amount from the daily
offerings,
With no one the wiser.
If money is Judas's motive,
Why kill its source?
The disciples say, "It was the money."
And this has waved in front of our eyes
Like a matador's cape.
But look behind the money;
Judas is not there at all.

Preacher There are minor notes, within the record,
That tend to verify your point.
Judas was, after all, one of the twelve,
A man honored by Jesus for special intimacy

And from whom he expected special service.
He was entrusted with the group's finances.
There is little to suggest that he was not
    trustworthy.
The Eastern Church has a tradition
That Judas was among the inner three or four
    disciples—
A member of the executive committee, if you please.
It makes sense.
Financial officers are generally included in decision
    making.
One account of the Last Supper
Suggests Judas was reclining close to Jesus,
Perhaps at the Master's side.
He and Christ spoke softly,
The others did not catch the drift of their
    conversation.
When he left abruptly,
They supposed he had been entrusted with a
    personal errand for Jesus.
The record does not contain much evidence
That Judas's behavior was suspect in any way,
Until that Gethsemane moment,
When he betrayed his Master with a kiss.

Advocate Precisely.
    So, let us begin from another point.
    Suppose it is his position of trust
    Which provides the clue to Judas's action.
    Imagine Jesus realizing that a confrontation with
      the establishment

Is inevitable . . . necessary . . . even the will of God.
Jesus wishes to choose the time and place for this
  encounter
So he can be ready, inwardly and outwardly, for the
  moment.
He selects an intimate and asks for his cooperation.
Judas will provoke the confrontation
According to Jesus' timetable.

Preacher But the kiss . . .
          To lead a man to death with a kiss.

Advocate Think of all the grieving relatives
          Who have kissed their beloved ones,
          Then instructed the life-support systems be
            unplugged.
          Remember the man mourning for his bride of fifty
            years,
          Her mind now hopelessly confused and Alzhei-
            merized.
          Did he not lovingly embrace her and kiss her fondly,
          Before he put the revolver to her head?

Preacher I see what you are suggesting.
          The kiss of death may not be treachery.
          It can be a symbol of love.
          But—then, why such great remorse
          If Judas is simply carrying out his Master's wishes?

Advocate His suicide may be an act of temporary madness.
          Overcome with anguish,

Having lost the one most precious to him.
Judas throws himself into death,
As the widow in suttee leaps upon her husband's
     funeral pyre.

Preacher   You would make our villain a hero of the cross.
           A large step, to be sure.
           Yet there is a rumor,
           It operates mostly underground within Western
                Christianity
           A sermon here . . . a novel there.
           The rumor suggests Judas may well have been the
                disciple
           Who most clearly understood Jesus' ministry.
           While Peter and the others seemed confused,
                baffled, bewildered,
           Until Easter cleared their vision,
           Judas, according to the rumor, knew right away
           Jesus' claim to be Messiah.

Advocate   He might have been the intellectual of the group.

Preacher   The rumor goes on:
           Steeped in the Old Testament Messianic tradition,
           Judas waits eagerly for the moment
           When Jesus will wipe off his lowly, meek disguise,
           Assume his power as Messiah,
           Raise an army, and drive the hated Romans into
                the sea.
           As the weeks and months go by
           Judas wonders about his friend.

Why doesn't Jesus take charge . . . assume command,
Step forth and claim his destiny?
Perhaps he needs assistance.
Judas will force Jesus' hand.
At the moment of his arrest,
Jesus will realize he must assume command,
Call upon the angels of Yahweh to protect Him,
Charismatically raise a people's army,
Subdue the enemy,
And raise the standard of the Kingdom of God.

Advocate   And, when Jesus did not assume power,
But instead adopted weakness as His weapon,
Allowing himself to be crucified,
Judas was overwhelmed with sorrow.
He did not intend his Master to be harmed.

Preacher   Can such great harm come from good intentions?

Advocate   Think of the inquisitors,
Torturing the body to save the soul.
Remember the crusades . . .
Wholesale slaughter for divine purpose.
Recall when you thought you were helping your
   children,
But you were actually hurting them.
Can great harm come from good intentions?
It happens every day.

Preacher   But the record speaks of treachery.
Not all people are at heart noble, you know.

Advocate   True indeed.
           But if treachery it was,
           Money was not the motive.
           An excuse at best.

Preacher   Perhaps there was a personal slight,
           An argument with Christ,
           The sense that another was taking his place as
               confidant and adviser.

Advocate   Perhaps a ruckus with the other disciples.
           One senses Judas was not well liked.
           He was not close to the others.
           Perhaps they circled,
           And he felt himself out of the loop.

Preacher   The house of treachery is often built brick by brick.
           Little disappointments,
           Slights real or imagined.
           The human mind builds mountains from molehills
               very quickly.

Advocate   Perhaps Judas sold his soul for revenge.
           It was not money.

Preacher   That leads us to the final question:
           Were you there?

Advocate   Or might we phrase it,
           "Is Judas here?"

Preacher   Which leads us to the ultimate question . . .

Both   For what will you sell your soul?

DEAR JESUS, WE DID
ENJOY THE PARADE, BUT . . .

John 12:19
"Look, the whole world has gone after him . . ."

Dear Jesus:
Just a quick note to let you know
How much we enjoyed the parade Sunday.
We thought the picnic was a wonderful idea.
Of course, the perfect weather helped.
It was such a treat to gather with you and the
    disciples,
There in the meadow . . .
And that chicken that Martha fixes . . .
Joan has got to get her recipe.
The kids had a lot of fun with the relay races and the
    ball game.
And when you got on that donkey . . .
I thought I'd split with laughter!
Hey, Clint Eastwood you ain't.
But it all worked out . . .
You riding into the city with your feet dragging
And the kids running beside you, waving palms . . .
Sweeping the road ahead of you,
Marching like drum majorettes, directing imaginary
    bands . . .
The rest of us got into it,
Laughing and singing and shouting

Our Hey sanna's and our Ho sanna's and our sanna
sanna Ho's.

I bet you were pleased with the turnout.
There were a lot of disciples there I hadn't seen for
a while.
And it really caught the attention of folks
Who were out for Sunday strolls or were just
hanging around,
Plenty of strangers and visitors,
And most of them seemed interested in what was
going on.
I thought your little speech at the city gate was good.
But I suggest going easy on the Messiah idea.
I realized the donkey and the parade pointed in that
direction.
But really, Jesus, you don't seem very Messiah-ish.
It just isn't you.
At least that's the way I see it.
Anyway, I think we made a breakthrough Sunday.
Folks are beginning to recognize you.
People are curious about your message.
You are being noticed.
The tough times are nearly over.

We had a wonderful time at the picnic and parade
Sunday.
I wish we could come to your supper Thursday,
And be with you Friday,
But we've made other plans . . . Sorry about that.
We'll call you Saturday . . .

This simple communion drama requires neither a formal set nor professional acting. It has introduced communion in retreat settings as well as small and large churches. It is most effectively presented by folks from the congregation who speak from the heart.

The celebrant (minister) begins the communion ritual with the appropriate words of institution and prayers. The communing begins with each actor coming forward and saying his/her part. Each is served by the celebrant. After "Legion" has spoken and been served, the congregation is then served. If it is appropriate, the actors may distribute the elements to heighten the impact of the drama.

The actors may wear a scarf or shawl or something simple to suggest biblical dress. The drama works that way. But it is equally, if not more, effective if folks dress in contemporary clothes according to their role.

I highly recommend typecasting. I hear over and over again from persons who have played Thomas, or Martha, or Peter and who have found the lines they spoke expressing their inner thoughts.

To date, I have been a part of this drama in nearly a score of different settings. I have heard from forty-five churches throughout the country who have used this drama—most during Holy Week. Folks tell me they were greatly moved by the service. That is my experience as well.

It is not often an author continues to be touched by his/her own words. This drama has worn very well for me; I am moved by it. In this case, I believe I got it right—and these words really become a vehicle of Grace. I pray you find it so.

AT THE TABLE

Peter

He said, "On rocks like you, Peter,
I am building my church!"

I can't understand it. Oh, when I'm high, I am
    terrific.
Some days I am ready for anything.
I feel like climbing Everest,
Swimming the Panama Canal;
I could tame a cage of hungry lions!
Some days I know that God
Could find no better servant
Than me, good old Peter!
I felt like that the day I said to Him,
"No matter what the others do,
You can count on me to the end!"
I meant it!
With every part of my being,
Every muscle, every nerve, every cell . . .
Oh, how I meant it!
I was high that day, I was up!
And the world was my oyster!

But, that night, in the courtyard,
It was so different.
Those soldiers were trying to get me
As they had Him.
I was scrambling for my life.
"I do not know Him," I said.
Over and over again, I said it,
"I do not know Him!"
"I do not know Him!"
Until that rooster split the air
With his awful cry,
And I knew I had done it again.

I had let Him down!
I was low that night,
Lower than a snake's belly.

That's the story of my life.
Like the girl in the poem,
When I am good, I am very, very good,
But when I am bad, I am horrid.
My feelings go up and down like a yo-yo.
Sometimes I feel . . .
I am living on a pogo stick.
And He said to me,
To this person with manic-depressive faith,
"On rocks like you, Peter,
I am building my church."

Celebrant Christ is for you, Peter.
You are accepted . . . when you are up,
When you are down.
Accept the fact you are accepted.
Take, eat, drink . . .
Christ is for you.

John

You know, I can't remember a time
When I did not feel a part of God's family.
It was the way we were raised.
God was a part of our home.
It always seemed very natural, when Dad said,

"John will return thanks,"
For me to verbalize the thoughts we shared together.
I don't suppose I have missed church
More than a dozen times in my whole life.
It just seems right to be here.
I can't imagine myself anywhere else.
I've always had a religious bent.
I've read the books and taken the courses.
I hold my own in theological debate.
That's why I was drawn to Him—at first.
I liked the way He put things.
He was simple, yet profound.
I knew I could learn in His presence.
And learn I did.
I suppose I can explain the meaning of who He was
About as well as anyone could.

At first His ideas attracted me.
But the more I was with Him,
The more my interest shifted.
I began to sense how He was treating people.
That man knew how to honor human beings!
He touched us all—the reprobates and losers,
Children, the wise, and the simple—
And we all were ennobled!
We left him walking taller
Than we had before.
He let us know we mattered
     To Him,
     To one another,
     To ourselves.

I came to Jesus seeking ideas,
And I received—love.
It's almost an obsession with me now.
A friend said, "John,
You are in love with love!"
Oh, I hope not,
Not that I don't want to be in love,
I do, desperately, want to be *in* love,
As He was *in* love.
I want to learn to love this whole wide world.
I want to honor and respect human beings
As did he.

Celebrant   Christ is for you, John.
            You are accepted in your loving quest.
            Accept the fact you are accepted.
            Take, eat, drink . . .
            Christ is for you!

Thomas

Every time I pass that painted rock, I get angry!
Years ago, someone scrawled
(In fluorescent color, no less)
"Christ is the answer!"
I keep hoping the paint will wear off.
It doesn't! . . . I suppose
The author of that Holy Graffiti
Retouches it from time to time.
The saying galls me . . .

"Christ is the answer!"
To what? What is the question?
I simply cannot understand folk
Who pluck answers off painted rocks.

"But, Thomas," my wife reminds me,
"Not everyone bears your convoluted mind."
She's right, of course.
I admit I overdo it.
My brain is forever thinking up another question,
A further implication . . .
I see three or four sides to issues
Which have only two.
She's right to call me on it.
I do get a kind of perverse pleasure
Out of being forever the skeptic, the doubter . . .
Blasting holes in pretty faith balloons.

Perhaps I overdo it;
But I will not apologize for my skepticism.
Land sakes, if we do not question,
We are not alive!
Look around; it's the people
Who get slogan answers
From painted rocks, or golden-tongued charismatics,
Who end up joining the flat-earth society,
Or drinking doctored Kool-Aid in the jungle.

He understood that.
He never put me down.

Oh, I know, sometimes,
My endless questions and speculations amused
    Him.
But he never turned off my brain.

I serve Him—tortured mind and all,
I remain more interested in questions
Than in slickly wrapped answers.
For once—no, often—
He reaches out his nail-pocked hand,
And we touch!

Celebrant   Christ is for you, Thomas.
             You are accepted in your believing
             And in your unbelieving.
             Accept the fact you are accepted.
             Take, eat, drink . . .
             Christ is for you!

Mary

I want to be here, but
I still don't feel comfortable in church.
The streets are my territory.
I was raised in the streets;
I plied my trade there for years.
I am at home with street people.

Churches are strange to me.
I hear the words, but . . .
I don't really understand them.

We are forever singing some "good old hymn"
That I have never heard before.

I never know what to say to church folks.
They seem nice enough;
But I can tell they feel awkward,
And so do I.
Sometimes I suspect, during coffee hour,
That someone behind me is pointing . . .
"There's Mary Magdalene,
The woman with the past."
It's probably all in my head.
Am I dressed right for church?
I can't get over the feeling
That church people get some kind of secret
     password,
Probably in Sunday school, when they are kids,
And from that time on
They know who really belongs.
What's the password?

I have the experience, of Him.
I understood his words,
Although he didn't really speak the language of the
     streets.
Maybe it was more his look—his touch.
I saw myself as honored, valued, useful.
When He said my name in that garden,
"Mary"
I knew I could never sell myself short again.

I don't suppose I'll ever help the church much.
It's in the streets where I can spread the news
Of what Christ did for me,
And what he waits to do for them.
I can talk to people in the streets;
If I have a "ministry," it's there, not here.

But I want to be with people who know Him.
I want the fellowship of those who love Him.
I need the people in church.
Perhaps they need me, too.
I just wish the church
Was a bit more like the street.

Celebrant Christ is for you, Mary.
You are accepted in the church as in the streets.
Accept the fact you are accepted.
Take, eat, drink . . .
Christ is for you!

Martha

I know I try to do too much.
He was right to bawl me out that day.
"Martha, you are distracted
By too much serving," He said.
Yes, I needed to relax a bit,
And catch my breath.
But you never heard Him complain
About my pot roast, did you?
And you should have seen the look on His face

When He put on the robe I made Him.
We understood each other, He and I.
He knew that dreamers like Him never get very far
Without someone around
Who knows how to sew on buttons!

I'd just as soon not be put on any more committees.
I've tried it.
Some folks thrive on all that talk
Of principles and objectives.
All I can think about
Is the work that is not getting done
While we sit around and talk.
Do all the talkers in the universe
End up in churches?

I'll spend *my* time, thank you,
Fixing the hinges, mowing the lawn,
Baking cookies, defrosting the refrigerator,
And fixing the leaky toilet.
And I'll probably get a bit cranky now and then,
'Cause I wonder why God made so few of us
Who notice dust and dirty windows.
If God really wants to bring in the kingdom,
God will raise up a few more folks
Who know how to use a rake and dustmop.

But I do get weary in my doing.
I need to be in touch with Jesus.
And I do appreciate the talkers
Who have planned this moment here with Him.

At this table,
I, who make a fetish out of serving,
Am served and nourished here.
It is hard for me, this quiet,
This opening-up . . . this taking . . .
But I am learning how to receive.

I am fed at this table. And afterwards?
You'll find me in the kitchen, of course.
The cups don't wash themselves, you know!

Celebrant Christ is for you, Martha.
You are accepted in your serving,
And in your receiving.
Accept the fact you are accepted.
Take, eat, drink . . .
Christ is for you!

Mother Mary

I'm learning to turn down those invitations to speak
To the women's association or the potluck dinner.
Those well-meaning church folks are getting to me.
I squirm at my introduction:
"*Mary, mother of the Lord!*"

People are beginning to ask me for my autograph!
They treat me like . . . a Ming vase!
Can you imagine how that makes a country girl feel?
The other day some woman asked me—get this—
She wanted my handkerchief!

To top it off,
When I catch myself in a mirror,
Off guard—you know the way it happens—
You're not deliberately looking in the mirror,
But you do and you notice yourself . . .
Maybe the way others see you . . .
And I realize—horror of horrors!
I am even beginning to look saintly!
(How did Mother Teresa stand it?)

Frankly, all this holiness is getting me down.
I wish the church would back off.
I gave Jesus life,
Joseph and I nurtured him in love,
But I am *not* a saint!
No way!

If I'd had my druthers,
He'd have died at 70 in his own bed,
Nazareth's beloved retired carpenter.
His son would have arranged the funeral.
The grandchildren would have cried.
We used to argue about that, Jesus and I.
I knew once He started preaching He was an
    endangered species.
"Come home," I pleaded,
"Come back to your tools, your work, your family.
Don't you love your family?"

He pointed to the riffraff around Him.
"This is my work . . . they are my family . . ."—

He held out his hands—". . . my tools."
He turned his back on me!
That hurt.
So do not call me a saint.
I was the mother of Jesus—*not* the mother of the Lord.
I fought *the Lord* every step of the way.

Until the end.
At the cross, the tears I wept as a mother
Mingled with the tears of those who wept for their
Lord.
I do not enjoy remembering those tears here at this
table.
A mother prefers not to dwell on her son's shed
blood and broken body.
Yet, here I am among those who remember Him,
And love Him, just as I.
And here this mother who cries out, "My Son!"
Feels supported by those who pray, "My Lord."

Celebrant Mother Mary, you are accepted
Accepted as the mother
Who stood by her Son from birth to death and
beyond.
You need not be nor act saintly.
You are accepted as Mary,
Accepted by that which is greater than you.
Accept the fact you are accepted!
Take, eat, drink—
Christ is for you.

Paul

"I received from the Lord
That which I also delivered unto you,
That the Lord Jesus on the night He was betrayed
Took bread . . ."

With these words this communion began.
They are my words;
I wrote them to the Church at Corinth.
And now, my words are used in every communion.
They are called, "Words of Institution,"
As though somehow the saying of them
Transforms a ceremony into a sacrament.
How ironic!

How ironic, indeed, that the church should so
     honor me
As to use my words at this most sacred time.
For most of my ministry I was suspect,
Perceived as a threat to the church
By the people who have just spoken;
The disciples, the women, the relatives . . .
The founders!

"Who is this Saul of Tarsus?" they cried,
"This outlander, daring to call himself *the apostle
     Paul!*
He is opening the church doors
To people who have no love, no respect,
No understanding of our tradition.
And this man never even met Jesus!"

That was the rub.
I had never known Jesus in the flesh.
Jesus, the human being.
That bothered *the founders*—
Peter, John, Jesus' brother James,
Mother Mary, Martha—all of them, really.
They could not understand
Why I dared speak of the mind of Jesus
When I had never met Him.

But I had met Him!!
Not the human Jesus,
The brother, rabbi, friend they knew,

But the Risen Christ!
The one who met me on that Damascus road
And changed my life forever!

I confess I confronted the founders.
Their love and devotion to Jesus in the flesh
Was condemning the church
To live in a Palestinian yesterday,
While I heard the Risen Christ
Calling to us from tomorrow,
Pulling us into all the world.

At this table, remember Jesus,
But do not dwell on the past.
Listen to the Risen Christ,
Feel the tug of His Spirit.
We Christians must go beyond the founders.

And, since mine are now the "Words of
    Institution,"
It appears I, the rebel, have now become *a founder!*
That's awful!
You must go beyond me!

You will!
As you follow where the Spirit leads!

Celebrant   Paul, you are honored here
For your allegiance to the Risen Christ,
And your courage to push the church into
    tomorrow.
Your insights are hallowed,
Your blind spots understood.
You are accepted,
Accepted by that which is greater than you.
Accept the fact you are accepted.
Take, eat, drink . . .
Christ is for you.

Legion

Call me Bartholomew,
Or Thaddeus, or Simon the Cananaean,
Or any of those disciples
Who are mentioned, then forgotten
By people who write Bibles.
Call me one of the three faceless Marys
Who appear in Holy Writ by first name only.
Call me Priscilla, or Phoebe,

Or the lost apostle, Matthias.
Call me, simply, *a man*, or *a woman*.
I am not overly significant to historians.
I'll never be elected Pope, or Stated Clerk,
Or anything like that.

My name is Legion.
We are Bill, Janet, Chris,
Harvey, Fred, Claudette, or Sally.
We are the bit players
In the drama of Holy History,
The supporting cast.
The program includes our names, nothing more.

But do not undervalue those names.
At some moment, God called my name;
And I responded, gave myself to God.
God knows my name!
And, at another moment, in some encounter,
God used my voice, my touch, my deed
To reach another human being.

That person knew my name . . . knows my name.
We shared a moment, He and I.
She and I met that moment in the Spirit.
Histories do not record these events,
But Kingdoms are built
By moments as we shared together.
I need not shout my name at this table.
God know it . . . knows me.
I come to be inspirited.

For who knows, perhaps this week,
Say Tuesday, at 3:45 p.m.,
The moment for which God nourishes me may
     come;
And I will sense the Spirit
Arcing from my extended hand
Into the heart of someone with a name
Like Bartholomew, or Clara, or Zeke!

Celebrant Christ is for you.
You are accepted, all you named and nameless ones,
Your names are known.
You are accepted,
Accepted by that which is greater than you.
Accept the fact you are accepted.
Take, eat, drink . . .
Christ is for you.

(*to the congregation*)

Friends, Christ is for you;
In your highs and lows,
In your loving and being loved,
In your belief and unbelief.

Friends, Christ is for us:
In the church and in the city,
In our serving and being served.
Friends, we are accepted; He knows our names.
Accept the fact we are accepted.
Take, eat, drink . . .
Christ is for us!

Easter morning worship often benefits from a switch in the regular routine. The following sermon comes at the beginning of worship rather than in the middle. As the congregation enters the sanctuary, the setting is predawn. The women have not yet arrived at the tomb. The sanctuary is dark and the organist plays somber music.

The bugler or trumpeter plays from the rear and is not seen by the congregation. The reader who begins the service with John's Easter account may be the same person as the Narrator, though it might be more dramatic to have different folk. Mary, Peter, and the Narrator may read from music stands—action is not needed.

When the sermon ends with the bugle playing reveille, the lights come on, the organist plays with gusto, and the congregation rises to sing the great Easter Hymn. The balance of the worship features hymns and anthems, scripture, prayers, communion—whatever is appropriate.

Perhaps it is wise to advise folk the week ahead that if they want to catch the sermon, they must be on time Easter morning—though it is more fun to have latecomers somewhat discombobulated.

THAT GREAT GETTIN' UP MORNING

The sanctuary is dark at the beginning. Lighting may be added gradually as the drama progresses—full lighting is needed at the end.

Reader   *Reads John 20:1–18*

Trumpet   *Plays taps*

As taps is played, the Narrator, Mary, and Peter take their places. They solemnly sing the opening words together.

All   (*sing—tune: taps*) Day is done.
             Gone the sun,
             From the lake, from the hills, from the sky.
             All is well.
             Safely rest.
             God is nigh.

Peter   God is nigh? I guess so.
             God is supposed to be nigh.
             Isn't that what we've all been taught?
             "Through thick and thin, God is nigh!"

             I cannot sing: "All is well."
             I will not sing it.
             All is not well. Not well at all.
             He is dead . . . executed . . . murdered.
             The best person I ever knew . . .
             He is dead,
             And I let it happen.
             I was so cocky and confident.
             I swore to Him,
             "You can count on me."
             I knew He was in trouble.
             I promised God I would protect Him.
             I was so certain I could see Him through.
             But I couldn't. I didn't.
             They killed Him.
             And I never lifted a finger . . .

Narrator   All is well, Peter.
             God is nigh.

Peter   All my life, since I was a kid,
             I've yearned for "All is well, God is nigh."
             I've always wanted my life to matter.
             I remember as a boy, lying under the skies at night,
             Looking up at the stars,
             I felt then God was nigh.
             I knew then that God, somehow, some way, knew I
                 was there.
             I wanted my "being there," "being here," to
                 matter . . .
             To God . . . to other people . . . to myself!

             Oh, I had dreams of doing great things for God
                 back then.
             But as time went on,
             It became obvious,
             My place in life was to be a fisherman,
                 Like Dad.
             "Well, all right," I said,
             "I'll be the best dang fisherman God ever made."
             And I was!

             Then He came to me . . . He called me . . .

Narrator   "Come, Peter, join me.
             We'll fish for people!
             Come help me build the Kingdom."

             You mattered, Peter . . . to Him.
             He said to you,
             "On rocks like you, Peter, I build my church."

Peter   How I wanted to be that rock.
               I wanted to be solid, firm, dependable.
               I wanted to matter.
               But it didn't work out that way.
               It's like my friend the fireman;
               I was kidding him one day about his soft job.
               He and his buddies sit around the firehouse most of
                   the time,
               Playing games, polishing the equipment, eating
                   gourmet meals . . .
               "Soft job," I said.

               "Yes and no," he answered.
               "There comes a moment when a child is trapped,
               The flames are about to reach her,
               And what I do in the next few seconds
               May mean life or death for her.
               I am trained to act in emergencies.
               The city pays me for sitting around,
               Just so I can be there at the moment that girl needs
                   help."
               He's right, of course;
               We gladly pay his salary
               So he can be there at that crucial moment.

               Well . . . my moment came,
               And I denied Him.
               Peter, the rock, turned into sand.
               The Master was counting on me,
               And I let Him down.
               I wanted my life to matter . . .
               It doesn't!

Trumpet   *Plays the last three lines of taps*

Mary   So now you know you don't matter, Peter.
            Welcome to the club.
            If you had been born a girl,
            You'd have known that long ago.
            We don't matter. We are a convenience.
            They teach us how to cook and sew,
            To keep a spotless house,
            How to clean a fish and kill a chicken.
            Then later on we learn just how to please a man.
            I learned well.
            A woman can make good money
            When she knows what men want.
            They'll pay for their convenience.
            But that's what we are—a convenience.
            We don't matter.

Narrator   Then you met Him, Mary.

Mary   And I was no longer a convenience.
            Not to Him! No one was.
            When He looked at me,
            Or talked with me,
            I became somebody . . . a person . . . Mary!
            It was not what I did or what I said.
            It was me, Mary . . . Mary was important.
            I found love with Him.
            And it was so different from what I had called love.
            We really ought to have another word for what He
                was,

And what He called forth in us.
Love is the best we can do.

But the word is so tainted . . .
Love does not seem big enough,
Not big enough to describe what we found in
   Him . . .
And He in us.
He knew me.
He spoke my name.
He cared.
And I understood love.

Narrator   Safely rest, Mary.
        God is nigh.

Mary   Is God nigh?
        There is no safe rest . . .
        A convenience knows too well.
        When they are through with you,
        They go off and leave you alone,
        Tossing and turning through the long nights.
        A convenience knows it is not safe . . .
        There is no rest.

        I thought His love would be different.
        Love never ends, they say.
        Oh, yes, it does!
        His love was too good for us.
        The world cannot stand such love.
        Love like His is killed, smothered, snuffed out . . .
           by death.

I loved . . . I lost.
Death won.
I toss and turn at night . . . alone.
Neither safe nor at rest.

Trumpet   *Plays last three lines of taps*

Narrator   God is nigh!
Get up, Mary.
Leave your troubled sleep, neither safe nor restful.
Pack up your spices,
And visit your loneliness.
Visit love in death's prison.
Notice the tomb, Mary.
Run, call Peter;
Tell him to bring his despair and come.
The rock is rolled away!
The tomb is empty.
He is not here!
Stand, Peter . . . Wonder, Mary.
He is not here!

Trumpet   *Plays the first four notes of reveille*

Narrator   Something is up.
Imagine the worst, Peter.
We all do.

Peter   They've stolen his body!

Narrator   Something is up.

Run off, Peter.

Stay, Mary, in that garden . . . wondering . . .
Embrace your loneliness.
Now . . . notice you are not alone.
Over there, standing in front of the rising sun . . .
See . . . someone is with you.
The gardener! He must be the gardener!

Mary   Sir, did you carry Jesus away?
         Where is his body?
         I wish to care for him.

Narrator Mary!

Mary   Teacher!

Trumpet *Plays first seven notes of reveille*

Narrator Something is up!
         Someone is up!
         Run, Mary! Find Peter!
         Tell him . . . tell the others . . . share the news
         Something is up!
         Someone is up!

Mary   I have seen the Lord!

Narrator Christ is risen!
         You matter, Peter.
         Your life matters.
         He will show you how and where.
         Put away your despair.

Christ is risen!
The grave does not snuff out love, Mary.
He will show you
How to go on loving,
How to live in love.
You need clutch your loneliness no longer.

Christ is risen!
Spread the news, Peter, Mary.
Tell the disciples, tell the others.
Tell us all
Who walk in darkness,
Who are alone,
And in despair.
Tell us bored ones,
Tell us who are giving up.
Spread the news.
Something is up!
Someone is up!

Mary and Peter go through the aisles, whispering:
Christ is risen. . . . Christ is risen, indeed.

As they reach the narthex, they shout out the front door:
Get up!
Get up, people of (*name of your city*)!
Christ is risen!
Christ is risen, indeed!

Narrator   It's that great gettin' up morning, friends.
Christ is risen,

And we are called to get up
And be with Him.

Trumpet   *Plays reveille (the whole thing)*

Organ immediately begins the introduction to "Jesus Christ Is Risen Today," and the congregation rises to sing it with great gusto!

While we all know the song "Dem Bones" and can sing it with enthusiasm, few of us realize the context. "Rev. Ezekiel" places the vision of the dry bones in the context of Ezekiel's life and gives a sense of the hopelessness he knew and felt. The congregation will readily join in the singing of "Dem Bones."

With a bit of encouragement, the verse at the end can be sung triumphantly and with a real sense of resurrection.

REV. EZEKIEL

Ezekiel 37:1–12; 24:15–18 (RSV)

Reader 1 Rev. Ezekiel, you know,
    Was born to be a priest.
    He had the calling.
    Why, as far back as anyone could remember,
    His family had been priests.
    He was raised in the temple
    And learned liturgical style
    At his daddy's feet (or uncle's)
    During all his growing-up years
    The dinner table conversation
    Explored the subtle nuances of ceremony
    And the niceties of temple ritual.
    He shone, as expected, at Jerusalem Seminary,
    Winning the senior prize,
    Settled down for a few years of priestly practical
     experience,
    Before pursuing his doctorate.
    And then the Holocaust struck.

Reader 2 Invading armies burned his city,
    Leveled his beloved temple,
    Subjugated his nation.

He was marched across the desert like a common
   criminal,
With a scraggly band of refugees,
Settled by a steamy Babylonian canal,
And expected to sing the Lord's song.

How does one sing the Lord's song
In a foreign land?
When beloved colleagues lie dead,
When God's Holy Temple stands in ruins,
When a promising priestly career is ended
And one is faced with obsolescence at age 25.
(There is little call for an expert in Temple Liturgics
In a community of Jewish sharecroppers
Tilling marshy Mesopotamian farmland.)
Welcome to the non-parish clergy, Rev. Ezekiel!

Reader 1   Well, he was not the first man (nor the last)
Who had to switch careers in midstream.
He learned to cope with farming,
Though he never felt it was his calling,
And gradually began to sense
He had a gift for preaching.
The folks around him picked that up.
It wasn't long before it was agreed,
No wedding, no family gathering, no community
   occasion was complete
Without a few words from Rev. Ezekiel.

That man could preach!
Oh, sometimes his preaching got out of hand.

Folks admitted they got rather tired
Of his gloom and doom numbers.
But they stuck it out,
'Cause no one ever knew
When he would get into the telling of his dreams.
My, that fellow had dreams!
Big, wonderful, Technicolor dreams!
And he could remember every little detail.
People wondered about that.
Did he write them down, or what?

Reader 2   His favorite dream was the one about the new
      temple.
He used to dream that one
Nearly every week.
It got so he could measure off the cubits
In every nook and cranny.
He drew a map and kept it on the bedside table.
He loved to preach about that dream . . .
How beautiful the temple would look.
How people would get back to worshipping God
The way it was supposed to be done;
How there would be a need for priests again,
People with his sort of liturgical training.
It was his favorite dream, all right.
Folks understood that.
And when they got around to putting all his
      preaching in the Book,
They spent a lot of pages on that dream,
Even though it meant more to him
Than to them (or us).

Reader 1   But there were other dreams, too,
            Marvelous, toe-tapping dreams,
            Just waiting for Fred Waring
            And every high school madrigal group that ever was
            To get their vocal chords around:
            (*sings*) "Ezekiel saw the wheel
            Way up in the middle of the air."

            (That's the number that comes just before the
                intermission.)

            And then for the finale, sing along:

            (*sings*) Dem bones, dem bones, dem dry bones
            Dem bones, dem bones, dem dry bones
            Dem bones, dem bones, dem dry bones
            Now hear the word of the Lord.

Reader 2   Now, when Rev. Ezekiel was preaching
            About those dreams,
            He didn't need to brighten them up
            With a kazoo, or a banjo, or a rattle,
            Like the madrigal singers do.
            Those dreams had more serious stuff to them
            Than we are likely to pick up
            At the spring music festival.
            Especially that dream about the bones.

Reader 1   It would be nice if we knew a lot more
            About the Rev. Ezekiel. . .

Whether he had kids, or played golf,
Or had any hobbies (other than his temple
    drawings).
We have to get our picture of the man
From what he said.
And one of the things he said
Certainly makes a person think.
It's tucked away in the middle of the Book,
Just a small paragraph in Chapter 24 . . . begins with
    verse 15 . . .
Gosh, a person could skip over it,
And never notice what Rev. Ezekiel said.

Reader 2   "The word of the Lord came to me:

    'Son of man, behold, I am about to take the
    delight of your eyes away from you at a stroke;
    yet you shall not mourn or weep nor shall
    your tears run down. Sigh, but not aloud;
    make no mourning for the dead. Bind on your
    turban, and put your shoes on your feet; do
    not cover your lips, nor eat the bread of
    mourners.'

    So I spoke to the people in the morning, and at
    evening my wife died. And on the next morning, I
    did as I was commanded."

Reader 1   Do you catch what the man says?
    "One morning," he says, "I went out preaching.
    I got home that night,
    And my wife—the person I cherish most in all the
        world—

Died in my arms.
And the next morning,
I went back to work!"

Come on, Rev. Ezekiel,
Haven't you read Kübler-Ross?
That stiff upper lip stuff went out with high-button
     shoes.
Don't give us this "word of the Lord" bit,
"Blessed are those who mourn . . .
They shall be comforted."
That's the word of the Lord.
Don't you hear Jesus?

Reader 2   But of course, he doesn't . . . didn't . . .
Back there . . . back then . . .
Way before Jesus.
Back then, the Rev. Ezekiel,
Born to be a liturgical expert,
Walked away from the ruins of his beloved temple.
The Rev. Ezekiel,
Born to cherish his beloved,
Walked away from the lifeless body of his wife.
And where else could he go
But back to work!

Reader 1   Where do you go?
Where do you go
When you hear for the hundredth time

On the six o'clock news
That another million people more or less
Are starving somewhere?
(Is it Africa this week?)
Where do you go
When you read of another rape,
Another drunken driver,
Another angry sect stockpiling weapons?
Where do you go when another friend
Comes down with cancer?
When another baby is found dead
In a trash bin?
Where do you go when . . .
Where is there to go
But back to work.

Reader 2   We're all back to work, Rev. Ezekiel,
Just like you.
Back to work . . . gives us something to do.
It keeps us from remembering.
Back to work . . . It's a narcotic.
We can block out the headlines.
Back to work . . .
We can forget the bloody scenes.
Submerge those awful feelings.
Back to work!

Reader 1   (*sings*) *Whistle while you work.*
We learn to do that.
But at night, we have those dreams,
The awful ones!

Like Rev. Ezekiel's.
He stood in the valley,
And dry, lifeless bones covered the ground about
     him.
He understood those dry bones:
His hopes were laid out on that valley floor:
          His dreams for his country,
          His yearning for his calling,
          His love.
Dry, dead bones.
He summed it up:
Our hope is lost!

Reader 2   Welcome to the club, Rev.

Reader 1   And then as he watched those bones
             Sinews . . .
             And flesh . . .
             And skin . . . brought those bones together.
             And the breath of God breathed on those bones.
             And Life appeared!
             And hope was reborn!
             And all the madrigal choruses in creation
             Sang with one voice.

             (*All join in, singing*)
             Dem bones, dem bones, gonna walk around,
             Dem bones, dem bones, gonna walk around,
             Dem bones, dem bones, gonna walk around,
             Now hear the word of the Lord.

Reader 1   Do you get that?
            Once more, with gusto . . .

            (*All sing*) Dem bones, dem bones, gonna walk around,
            Dem bones, dem bones, gonna walk around,
            Dem bones, dem bones, gonna walk around,
            Now hear the word of the Lord.

Reader 2   Ezekiel's God, we pray we might
            Feel breath upon our dreams tonight!

"Rev. Ezekiel and the Half Flood" lifts up one of the great but often neglected images of the Bible. Many in the congregation will be hearing it for the first time. The second reader is primarily a singer in this dialogue. The song is a familiar folk hymn (#350 in The Presbyterian Hymnal) *and can be done a cappella or accompanied by guitar or organ. At the end, the congregation joins in the song.*

This is appropriate at services featuring baptism. It also has an ecological twist and would be welcome on Earth Day or at times when the church celebrates God's world and our stewardship.

REV. EZEKIEL AND
THE HALF FLOOD

Psalm 137; Ezekiel 47:1–12

Reader 1   The sermon was about Noah and the ark and the
                  rainbow
              That dry, dry Sunday morning during the drought
              That nearly brought the county to its knees.
              At prayer time, someone said,
              "I don't know if we would want a full-on flood,
              But we sure could use half a flood . . ."
              And the preacher prayed for one that day.
              That's the image in the scripture today.
              It is the marvelous vision of Rev. Ezekiel,
              About the Temple and the half flood.

              Rev. Ezekiel was meant to be a priest.
              He is born into a family
              Where his daddy and granddaddy
              And all the great granddads anyone can remember
              Have been priests, serving God in the temple.

And just when Ezekiel finishes his theological training
And is ready for full-time temple service,
His country is overrun by a conquering army;
His beloved temple is destroyed,
He and his kin are forcibly resettled
On marginal Mesopotamian farmland
Around present-day Iraq.

Those were tough, tough times
For people who thought of themselves as God's People.
They couldn't understand why . . .
Why had God deserted them?
They wrote and sang
Their sad, sad laments
We can read them in the Bible today.

Reader 2   "By the Rivers of Babylon,
            There we sat down and there we wept
            When we remembered Zion.
            On the willows there,
            We hung our harps.
            For there our captors asked us for songs
            And our tormentors asked for mirth,
            Saying, 'Sing us one of the songs of Zion!'
            How could we sing the Lord's song in a foreign
                land?"

Reader 1   Rev. Ezekiel learned how . . .
            How to sing the Lord's song in a foreign land.

> 'Cause he started dreaming big dreams,
> And when he got to telling people about them
> Those great big, wonderful, Technicolor dreams,
> Well, his telling about them was so marvelous,
> It seemed like singing,
> So folks just naturally joined in.

Reader 2   (*sings*) Ezekiel saw the wheel way up in the middle of the air . . .
Ezekiel saw them dry bones . . .

Reader 1   And one of his greatest dreams was about the temple and the half flood.
But as far as we can tell,
No one has written a song about it yet.
But if you have ever lived through a drought,
Ever been rationed to fifty gallons a day,
You'll find this dream in Ezekiel 47:1–12
A wonderful passage.

Reader 2   (*sings*) Fill my cup, let it overflow,
Fill my cup, let it overflow,
Fill my cup, let it overflow,
Let it overflow with love. (*Hum as scripture is read*)

Reader 1   Listen for the word of God. (*Read Ezekiel 47:1–12*)

Reader 2   (*sings*) Let it overflow with love . . .

(*speaks*) That's a beautiful picture . . .
The temple becomes the source of life.

Sweet, fresh, potable water
Flows out over the land . . .
Stagnant water becomes fresh,
Fish thrive, trees become heavy with exotic fruit,
The garden of Eden returns.

Reader 1   Did you notice the part
About the swamps and marshes remaining salty?
"Aha!" shout the environmentalists among us.
"God saves the wetlands and marshes;
Why can't we?"
You can almost hear them shouting,
"Rev. Ezekiel for County Supervisor!"

Reader 2   God's waters, which touch us at baptism
Marking us forever as God's own person,
Now flow out to soak and nourish the land.
God's covenant leads to Abundant Life.

Reader 1   Remember that early covenant
Made by God with Israel?
"I shall be your God. You shall be my people."
That was the basic covenant relationship at Sinai.
Why did God choose those particular people?
Were they a genetically superior people?

Reader 2   (*sings*) Fill my cup, I'm so wonderful . . .

Reader 1   Were they more righteous than others?

Reader 2   (*sings*) Fill my cup, I deserve it more . . .

Reader 1   Did God choose them because they were so
           attractive?

Reader 2   (*sings*) Fill my cup, I'm so lovable . . .

Reader 1   No way!
           The point of the covenant is in that overflowing . . .
           Israel is a chalice . . . a cup,
           Into which God pours living, healing, abundant
              waters.
           God pours and keeps pouring and then pours some
              more,
           Until the chalice overflows.
           The waters spread out to cleanse, to nourish, to
              renew the earth;
           The covenants of God are for the whole world.

Reader 2   "God so loved the world
           That God gave the only begotten son
           That whoever believes in Him
           Should not perish, but have eternal life."

           "I am come," said the Master,
           "That you may have life
           And have it abundantly!"

Reader 1   Exactly!
           And if we ask,
           How may we keep covenant with God?
           How do we live up to our side of the relation-
           ship?

The Bible answers:
God provides the energy.
God's living water keeps flowing from the temple.
As long as we are in touch with God,
Responsive to God's Word,
That living water just keeps on coming,
Keeps on healing, keeps on renewing.
And the only way it gets blocked is
If we get greedy.

Reader 2   (*sings*) Fill my cup . . . and leave the bottle.

Reader 1   Or stingy.

Reader 2   (*sings*) Fill my cup . . .and mine alone!

Reader 1   Or unresponsive to God's Word.

Reader 2   (*sings*) Fill my cup . . . and cut out the advice.

Reader 1   That's when we run out of energy,
             When faith seems a burden,
             And God becomes a bother.

             But bother us God will. That is part of the promise.
             When covenant people get out of touch,
             God sends forth prophets
             To call us to faithfulness.

Reader 2   (*sings*) Fill my cup, let it overflow,
             Let it overflow with love.

Reader 1   (*Reader 2's first name*), child of the covenant,

Reader 2   (*Reader 1's first name*), child of the covenant,

Reader 1   (*to the congregation*)
             You, all of you . . .
             Us, all of us . . .
             Children of the covenant
             The waters of baptism . . . our baptism.

Reader 2   The healing waters from the temple.

Reader 1   God's abundant living waters.

Reader 2   God's covenant baptismal waters are for you! For us!

Reader 1   "And the water flows from the Temple
             And waters all the earth
             And goes down into the Arabah,
             And the sea of stagnant waters becomes fresh,
             And there are many fish
             And all kinds of trees for food,
             And the waters are for healing . . ."

Reader 2   (*as the above is read, Reader 2 sings . . .*)
             Fill my cup, let it overflow,
             Fill my cup, let it overflow,
             Fill my cup, let it overflow.

             (*Reader 1 joins in the last line*)

Both   Let it overflow with love.

(*The readers and congregation sing together:*)
Fill my cup, let it overflow,
Fill my cup, let it overflow,
Fill my cup, let it overflow,
Let it overflow with love.